16.95
N

DATE DUE / DATE DE RETOUR

DEC 19 1992		
JUL 28 1993		
MAY 21 1994		
JAN 10 1995		
NOV 29 1995		
APR 18 2000		
APR 19 2000		
OCT 9 2001		
DEC 27 2005		

CARR McLEAN   38-297

Symbol of the pioneer spirit and steadfast rural values: a grain elevator in Saskatoon in the province of Saskatchewan.

DESTINATION
CANADA

Photographs: Harald Mante
Text: Harald R. Fabian
Karl Teuschl

WINDSOR BOOKS
INTERNATIONAL

"Pumpkin parade." A farm on the St. Lawrence River between Montreal and Québec presents its harvest produce for sale.

CONTENTS

The fishing village of Percé on the Gaspé Peninsula with the 100-metre-high Percé rock offshore.

...AND WAY BEYOND THE HORIZON IS CANADA

Here – Where is That?

There is a large Santa Claus toy production facility lying north of Alert, but otherwise nothing. The factory's head office is at the North Pole and HOH OHO is the postal code used by the primarily English-speaking children of Canada when they send off their lists of wishes to Father Christmas.

Every year, Alert has 145 days of never-ending darkness and an equally long period of continuous summer sunlight. Lying on the northeastern coast of Ellesmere Island in Canada's Northwest Territories, it is the northernmost settlement in the world. From there, it is only some 830 kilometres to the North Pole. The community serves as a defensive Early Warning Station, air force base, joint Canada-United States weather station, and is manned by around two hundred employees.

Windsor, at the tip of the land strip separating Lake Huron and Lake Erie, has a population close to one quarter of a million people. Here the Detroit River marks the border between the province of Ontario and the American state of Michigan. The industrial cities of Windsor and Detroit are connected by both a tunnel and the Ambassador Bridge. Cars are produced on both sides of the river. American ones.

Alert and Windsor, Canada's southernmost city, are more than 4,500 kilometres apart and are separated by more latitudinal degrees than Norway's North Cape is from the Greek island of Crete in the Mediterranean. Between the two, there lies what the author Mordecai Richler has ironically called "home, sweet home", or "the unknown and unfinished country" as the journalist Bruce Hutchison has affectionately criticized it. And it is indeed that for the majority of Canadians. With an area of some 9,98 million square kilometres, it is as large as the European land mass from the Atlantic to far beyond Moscow. Its population slightly exceeds that of California or is less than half of Britain's, numbering just over twenty-five million. Sixty percent of the population is concentrated in just the two provinces of Ontario and Québec, while a mere 0.2 percent occupy the Northwest Territories, an area larger than India and comprising one-third of Canada.

If in Europe you were to drive from Lisbon to Moscow, you would cover some five thousand kilometres and cross at least half a dozen national borders – and just as many linguistic ones. Anyone driving the Trans-Canada Highway from the Atlantic to the Pacific, from St. John's in Newfoundland to Victoria in British Columbia, would travel through ten Canadian provinces. He would cross the Appalachians, shaped by millions of years of ice and water, in Newfoundland, Nova Scotia, on Prince Edward Island and in New Brunswick; the narrow, fertile lowlands of the St. Lawrence River in Québec; the forest and lake landscapes of the Pre-Cambrian Canadian Shield in Ontario; the prairie grainlands in Manitoba, Saskatchewan and Alberta; the Rocky Mountains and the Cordilleras in British Columbia. He would pass through five time zones. Five thousand kilometres would bring him to Winnipeg leaving yet another twenty-five hundred kilometres to travel.

To fly from Montreal, Toronto, Edmonton or Vancouver to Frobisher Bay, Resolute or Tuktoyaktuk in the Northwest Territories is to travel into a vast emptiness. You would fly northwards from the densely populated strip along the Canada-United States border into Arctic regions, where tiny settlements cower on the ground and where the population density is still not a measurable whole number. You would fly over rivers and streams where ice can support heavy trucks; over lakes that could well swallow Massachusetts or the whole of Yorkshire; over regions as extensive as a European country – yet devoid of all infrastructure, be it road, rail or power transmission lines, and which remain untouched by the plough; over tundra where gigantic caribou herds roam hundreds of kilometres without once approaching any human settlement. Hours later, when the plane would finally land in Frobisher Bay

The Gros Morne [Nati]onal Park [on] the west coast of [the Island of [N]ewfound-[lan]d is one of [the] region's most [fa]scinating areas of [un]touched nature.

9

or Resolute, somehow or other it would seem to be rather smaller than when it took off.

"Où suis-je? Ici – Où ça? Ici – Où ça?" This question, posed by the Montreal author Claude Péloquin, is a plea for comprehensible frame of reference in a vast and empty country with the dimensions of a continent: "Where am I? Here – but where is here?" According to the literary critic Northrop Frye, Canadian consciousness is puzzled less by the question "Who am I?" than by such an enigma as "Where is here?" Here is just somewhere.

Visiting Chisasibi

We were on the way to James Bay. Alain was driving. He had a hangover and yawned frequently. Sylvie was joking with us, her companions. Alain was speeding across the Province of Québec's taiga. We were close to the 54th Parallel and it was a cool blue-grey morning in June.

The black spruce beside the gravel highway seemed prematurely aged and tough, their trunks hardly thicker than ten to fifteen centimetres. They stood interspersed with shrubbery, alder and larch. From the top of a rise we could survey the flat rolling

taiga. Three or four pickup trucks passed us, the men in the passenger cabins wearing overalls and safety helmets. A helicopter flew for a while parallel to the road and then from time to time circled around a tower supporting the overhead transmission cables that supply power to Chisasibi. Not a single bird was to be seen. Now and again it rained.

I was thinking of Stevie on Vancouver's West 47th Avenue, of the lawn in front of her house and of the good coffee she prepared for her Bed & Breakfast guests. I was recalling the response "Oh, is that right!" that she inevitably made to all observations. At this hour in Vancouver it would be shortly after six o'clock in the morning, three hours earlier than in Québec. Maybe Stevie was just getting up.

And I recalled flying with Ted Grant from Fort Simpson to Nahanni National Park in the Northwest Territories. Also on board had been a couple with their small daughter. The man had been busy filming with his raspberry-coloured video camera, his wife sitting silently. Ted had flown the family to Little Doctor Lake, where their lonely log cabin stood beside a narrow lakeside beach and where, plagued by horse flies, we had gathered strawberries. From the shoreline, the man had filmed us taking off from the

lake, with mother and daughter standing close together off to one side. Silent.

We needed a good hour for the hundred or so kilometres from Radisson to Chisasibi. The Cree Indian village at the mouths of La Grande Rivière in James Bay wasn't old. The residents had moved in not quite seven years before. Their former village, Fort George, had been situated on an island in the river mouth. But the island had been threatened by erosion. In 1979, the most powerful of three hydro-electric power plants along La Grande had gone on line at Radisson, making the average current in the lower reaches twice as strong as before. In 1981, the residents of Fort George – numbering some two thousand Cree and several Inuit and Whites – had moved with all their worldly goods over to the south bank of the river. The Cree had laid out the new village as they saw fit, with some three dozen groups of houses centering on a hospital, school, sports hall, general store and various administrative buildings. The size of the clusters corresponded to the size of the family clans. Four years after the village had been established, it had been necessary to reinforce the river bank beside Chisasibi with thousands of cubic metres of gravel.

Alain drove into the centre of town. He wanted something from the store. Sylvie and I went to the cafeteria and drank two weak coffees in paper cups. The day before, Sylvie had eagerly led me on a guided tour that took us over dams and dykes, through turbine galleries and down into subterranean construction sites. The power stations along La Grande enthralled her, the erection of a high tension mast the very stuff of high drama. Sylvie was studying mechanical engineering in southern Québec and worked part-time in Radisson as a tour guide.

Alain returned with some metal object under his arm that looked like the elbow of a stove pipe. We continued on to the bakery. On our way here, Sylvie and Alain had been singing the praises of "Baker Cree". The smell of baking wafting our way made our mouths water. We purchased a few doughnuts for our trip. They were still warm and had been well sprinkled with icing sugar. Outside it was drizzling. We drove out of the village past simple detached houses and onto a narrow track leading westwards. After less than ten kilometres we reached James Bay. The track ended in low-lying dunes of light-grey sand and stubby undergrowth. Snowmobile wrecks littered the area. Overturned boats were lying on the

11

bank. Strewn everywhere were red shotgun cartridges. A dull grey surface extended to the horizon, – placid, undisturbed. Alain tossed a few stones into the water.

I recalled a waterscape painted by some nameless adherent of the school of realism. I had seen it hanging in a gallery in Yellowknife. A wooden landing stage at the lower edge of the picture directed the viewer's gaze upwards to a single-engine seaplane. A fuel canister stood on the dock. An icy blue sky filled the upper half of the picture – a sky seemingly behind glass. Pale green tundra extended beyond the lake. Yet further away, there had been nothing. That was Canada. The plane would fly for hours and land on another lake, take off again and land again. And far beyond the horizon would still be Canada.

The expanse of water in front of us was empty. We started back. Sylvie and Alain wanted to drive me to the airstrip near Radisson. It was my last day on La Grande. We ate the doughnuts. I visualized Henry Hudson as he stared emptily ahead, his eyes blank. That's how some fictional account, encountered somewhere and vaguely remembered, had depicted this English sailor. A man bereft of all hope, in an open boat surrounded by icebergs, his adolescent son at his feet. In 1611, after enduring a winter on James Bay, his crew had mutinied and set them adrift. Hudson, his son and seven sorrowful companions, were never seen again.

Twenty years later, Thomas James had wintered in the same bay. He returned to England certain of one thing: this was neither the route to East Asia nor the Northwest Passage sought by him and by so many before him. The bay was named after him. Four or five decades later, fur traders were regularly crossing James Bay. The Hudson's Bay Company, following its foundation in London in 1670, had set up trading posts at the mouths of the rivers that flow into the Hudson Bay and James Bay: Fort Prince of Wales, York Factory, Fort Severn, Fort Albany, Rupert House, Eastmain House. Garrisons for the fur trade. In Europe, beaver fur hats and muffs had become the latest fashion, status symbols for the nobility and clerics, for officers, snobs and ladies of society. Meanwhile, in North America, people were dying in skirmishes fought to win control of the fur trade. Top quality beaver pelts became the accepted unit of currency in barter trade with Indians: each was the equivalent of a gallon of brandy, a brass cauldron, or a pair of shoes.

The scheduled flight to Montreal had been delayed, but nobody in Radisson's small airport was getting upset. Most of them knew each other. Almost all of them were employed keeping "Québec Dynamo" on La Grande operating.

Filling the West

It was a pleasant summer day in Alberta. White clouds against a blue sky. Geese could be heard gobbling. A little girl in a dark dress, her hair tied up in a black and white polka dotted scarf, pointed up at a tower, ten or twelve metres high that supported a water tank. "D'you want to climb up there?" she asked. I didn't and claimed that I was afraid of heights. "I've often climbed up there, but I shouldn't," she announced without a trace of distrust, proud but also slightly embarrassed.

We were visiting one of the communal farms owned by the Hutterites in Alberta, almost midway between Calgary and Edmonton. The tower would provide a good view and I knew that one would see grain growing in flat fields rolling away forever to the horizon, criss-crossed by backroads and highways, with the larger communities' white, red or green silos catching the eye. There were grain elevators lined up beside the railway tracks, and at the edge of the cultivated expanses, white farmhouses stood with brightly painted eaves, door and window frames. Now, outside of harvest time, this scenery induced a soothing serenity.

A farmer's wife had told me about the farm. Her husband had spoken disparagingly about the Hutterites' habit of always paying cash, even for larger purchases, with dollars accumulated in a common fund. The farmer, a descendant of Irish immigrants, didn't hold with "all this Christian communism," or with the Hutterites' absolute rejection of bearing arms even in times of crisis. However, his wife regularly bought eggs from them.

Our little climber, accompanied by two somewhat older girlfriends, was allowed by her parents to show me around the settlement. The road was bordered by plain dormitories on the one side and by buildings comprising the slaughter house, bakery, communal kitchen and dining hall on the other. I was also taken to the house where eggs are sorted and where other young girls – abashed and giggling at the appearance of strangers, but still curious – were just cleaning up. Then I was shown the vegetable garden, the schoolhouse and the large workshop used for repairing the agricultural machinery brought in by neighbouring farmers. Some seventy Hutterites were living and working here in accordance with their beliefs, shunning all worldly luxuries since for them

*d blossoms
a Niagara-
n-the-Lake
aid a large
it-growing
area
uthwest of
onto. This
agnificent
display is
ly a short
ance from
celebrated
waterfalls.*

13

View of the luxurious Hôtel Château Frontenac in Québec City.

such extravagances are worshipped only by idolaters. The three girls stood puzzled when asked whether they ever drove into the city. The eldest finally answered, stating they visited their uncles and aunts on other Hutterite farms.

In earlier days, the prairie provinces of Alberta, Saskatchewan and Manitoba offered enough space for all newcomers: religious minorities such as the Doukhobors, Hutterites, Mennonites and Mormons; Germans and Ukrainians, Icelanders and Hungarians, Norwegians, the Dutch and Americans; the persecuted, displaced and outcast. In the decades that followed the signing of the British North America Act, by the provinces of New Brunswick, Nova Scotia, Ontario (Upper Canada) and Québec (Lower Canada) and thus forming the Dominion of Canada in 1867, thousands streamed onto the prairies. They were lured by the prospect of a new and dignified existence as settlers in a free and open country.

Around 1870, the region between Winnipeg and the Rocky Mountains was occupied by some 40,000 people, more than three-quarters of whom were Indians and Métis, the descendants primarily of white trappers and Indian mothers. Thirty years later, the population in this region had increased more than tenfold. The fifteen years leading up to the First World War saw the greatest wave of immigration. More than three million people streamed into the Dominion as a result of an aggressive immigration policy designed to populate the country, and above all, the prairies. The Mennonites founded Steinbach in Manitoba, the Mormons Cardston in Alberta, the Hungarians Esterhazy, the Dutch Edam in Saskatchewan and the Icelanders Gimli on Lake Winnipeg. Ukrainians settled in and around Edmonton and in southeastern Manitoba, Doukhobors at Yorkton in Saskatchewan, and Hutterites at Lethbridge in Alberta. Germans, who today comprise the third largest group in Canada's ethnic mosaic after those of British and French descendancy, gave their new homes such names as Schoenwiese, Schanzenfeld and Blumenort. They all brought with them hopes for a better future. They were to be Canada's own future.

Dominion-status attracted new settlers. In 1870, Manitoba joined confederation, in 1871 British Columbia and in 1873 Prince Edward Island. Canada, which in 1867 had been limited to the two coastal provinces in the east and the region from the Great Lakes to the Gulf of St. Lawrence, – an area close to 907,000 square kilometres and inhabited by 3.5 million people – now stretched from the Atlantic to the Pacific. But between Manitoba, which at its foundation comprised only a fraction of the present-day province, and British Columbia, there was a vacuum. A virtually deserted territory extended from the Hudson Bay up to the Rocky Mountains, known as Rupert's Land. In 1670, England's King Charles II had passed this area into the sole charge of the Hudson's Bay Company in return for a symbolic rent: namely, that whenever a British monarch after 1670 set foot on Rupert's Land, the fur-trading company had to present him with the pelts of two elks and two beavers. Only on four occasions has this been called for, the last time being in 1970 when Queen Elizabeth, in the vicinity of Winnipeg entered the erstwhile Rupert's Land.

In 1869, for 1.5 million dollars the Hudson's Bay Company sold back to the British Crown the entire territory, an area which comprised about forty percent of present-day Canada and which included – apart from today's Northwest Territories – also parts of Ontario and Québec. This transaction confronted Canada with the problem of settling the prairies and of joining up provinces lying far apart. People had to be encouraged to settle the west. In return for a single payment of ten dollars, homesteads of almost sixty-five hectares were promised to those Europeans and Americans who were prepared to break the land, with the sole condition being that the homestead be cleared and cultivated. In 1881, only a little more than one million hectares of the prairie provinces were being farmed. But fifty years later, over forty-four million hectares were arable. At this time, Canada was developing into one of the world's largest grain producers.

There were, however, other reasons underlying the systematic encouragement of settlement, this so-called "filling the west". During the nineteeth century, the United States and British North America had been embroiled in a number of military conflicts. For instance, in 1812, the Americans, seeing their merchant shipping and their lucrative export trade to Europe jeopardized by the Continental Blockade, declared war on Britain and therefore, on Britain's colonies in North America. Fighting continued until 1815 to determine who should control the territory around the Great Lakes. This pitted Americans and United Empire Loyalists against each other, the latter being those Americans who had maintained allegiance to the British Crown by fleeing to the British-Canadian colonies after the American War of Independence.

Old animosities flared up yet again during and after the American Civil War. Officially, the British claimed to be neutral in the conflict while in point of fact, favoured the American secessionist southern states by

*"Petit
Champlain",
the oldest
part of
Québec City
the Place
Royale, is still
aware of its
eighteenth
century
heyday.*

17

The Samu *de Champ* *monumer* *erected in* *Québec C* *faces the* *Hôtel* *Château* *Frontena* *Here in 1* *he found* *the tradin* *post that* *the follow* *centuries* *to develo* *into toda* *modern c*

providing safe havens for Confederate shipping in Canadian ports. Many in the United States would have been ready to encourage the annexation of the British colonies, while many Canadians became seriously concerned that the victorious and now unemployed northern armies of the United States would invade.

Indeed, the years 1866 to 1871 saw a number of military attacks initiated by a radical Irish-American association, the Fenian Brotherhood, with the aim of conquering Canada. All this encouraged the new Canadian federation to settle quickly the new territories, to build a defensive corridor against the feared Yankee attempts to effect annexation. Nowadays Canada's most important trading partner is the United States, the so-called "Big Brother" lying south of the 49th Parallel, which since 1846 has marked the Canada-United States border all the way from the Great Lakes to the Pacific Coast.

Since Confederation in 1867, Canada has absorbed over eleven million immigrants, five million of whom arrived following World War II. Now it is no longer Hutterites and Mennonites that arrive, and the number of immigrants from Europe is on the decline. Rather, it is immigration levels from the crisis-stricken regions of Asia, Africa and Central America that are increasing. Canada also anticipates many Chinese immigrants towards the end of the millennium at which time Britain's lease on Hong Kong expires. These newcomes will not settle on the prairies, but rather in British Columbia, where in Vancouver a large Chinatown already exists.

Prince George for Instance

Steve bore a considerable resemblance to the shoes he was repairing. They sat up on shelves on the wall behind him. Bulky work boots, with thick soles, stiffened toes bent upwards, and the upper leather full of ridges and cracks reflecting hours of work over months and years.

Steve's wrinkled face was a reminder of a lifetime of work. Twenty-five years earlier, he had come from Hungary to British Columbia. He still spoke English with a strong accent. But now he had a shop on George Street, Prince George's main thoroughfare, with the train station at one end and the townhall at the other. His granddaughter spoke with no trace of an accent. She was helping him out in the store. Steve sewed a torn strap and charged two dollars.

There are many shops like "Steve's Shoe Repair" in Prince George. The forests and the allowed annual cut are the town's basis for existence. The lumber industry supports fifteen sawmills, three paper and cellulose factories, a plywood factory and the two chemical works that supply the paper mills with bleach and adhesive additives. Many work boots suffer due wear and tear in Prince George.

Each year, here in British Columbia's largest forest region, there are some eight and a half million cubic metres of timber to be felled, transported, processed and consigned. Heavily laden logging trucks are to be seen throughout the region transporting great lengths of lumber. Tree trunks are piled high in the lumber yards belonging to the saw mills along the Fraser River. At the two principle freight depots, freight cars loaded with freshly cut beams and planks are lined up in long queues awaiting transport.

Prince George offers little reason to stand and stare. No old churches, no architectural gems, no impressive art collections or museums, and no out-of-the-ordinary panorama. A town that is the stuff of no one's dreams. It is a town like many in Canada: spread out, tailored to the automobile, with a few ten or twelve storey apartment blocks, hotels and office towers, unadorned commercial premises and a square of shop fronts. On the outskirts is an expanse of detached houses.

The picture is similar in Kamloops and Fort Saint John, in the agricultural centres of the prairie provinces, and in Whitehorse in the Yukon Territory. They are towns that make claims on no one but rather wait to be claimed and to fulfil their function as shopping, supply and service centres. Honest, respectable, and practical towns – nothing more and nothing less. You forget them as soon as you move on, and then recognize them later – still further down the road.

Prince George is younger than the trees being felled in vicinity. The process of development that has made it British Columbia's third largest town dates from the decade that preceded the First World War, when plans for a second trans-Canadian rail link were formulated. The new line would carry passengers and freight from the Pacific coast, via the Yellowhead Pass in the Rocky Mountains, through Edmonton and Saskatoon onto Winnipeg, allowing journeys to continue on to Moncton in New Brunswick.

The first railway to connect the Atlantic with the Pacific had been completed already in 1885, facilitating and promoting the settlement of Canada's southern expanse. It provided the decisive impulse that promoted the development of Kamloops, Calgary and many other towns along its line.

The primary purpose underlying the second transcontinental railway system was to connect the northern prairie regions – namely those in the provinces of Alberta and Saskatchewan, where the population had been considerably augmented by the arrival of the Europeans – with eastern Canada and the new Pacific port of Prince Rupert. The reports of the plan for a new rail were enought to vitalize the area where the Nechako flows into the Fraser River and where the nineteenth century fur-trading post of Fort George had stood. While at the beginning of this century only a few hundred Indians had been living on a reservation, by 1910, two small settlements of some two hundred inhabitants each had been established – and the first white woman arrived. Several sawmills were built. In 1912, the Grand Trunk Pacific Railway bought the site that the Indian reservation occupied and commissioned a Boston architectural firm to design a town on the site. In 1914, the year that witnessed the linking of the railroads from the east and west, the first houses were in place, and in the following year, the new community adopted the name of the then Prince of Wales.

At the beginning of the 1960s, Prince George was home to almost 14,000 residents. Then the boom years arrived. Paper and cellulose companies moved in and set up factories. The town spread outwards, its population multiplied fivefold and its per capita income was, for a time, the fourth highest in Canada. From every direction those looking for work converged on Prince George. For British Columbia it became "the hub of the north".

Sam too had arrived at that time. I met him one evening in the bar of the hotel just across from Steve's Shoe Repair. Previously he had been in Vancouver and we chatted a bit about that city – enthused, of course, about the unique beauty of Vancouver's setting on the English Bay, about its abundance of air and light and water, its green, warm, bright light, not a trace of winter, a feast for the eye.

"I changed my life and my wife and everything," said Sam. Now he was the hotel's restaurant manager and in his spare time, he usually drove off to go fishing in the great outdoors. Or he constructed cupboards and wooden chests. Almost everybody around the town was involved in some way with wood. Sam told me that he lived in a good area of Prince George, up in the hills and, on most days,

usually well clear of the emissions spewed out by the industrial plant.

But when unfavourable winds blow, Prince George has its own individual smell, that of a town in which wood oils and construction timber are produced for the United States, pinewood furniture for Scandinavia, chopsticks for Japan and pre-fabricated log cabins for Canada and the world.

Do You Know Kerouac?

"Vous connaissez Kerouac?" Louis Dussault appeared surprised at my question. In the waiting room to his office he found a comprehensive dossier containing all the press cuttings about an international meeting in honour of Jack Kerouac held in October 1987. It had brought together writers, professors, biographers, friends and colleagues of Kerouac, including Allen Ginsberg and Lawrence Ferlinghetti, in Québec City. Louis Dussault, Director of the *Secrétariat permanent des peuples francophones,* (Permanent Secretariat of French-speaking Peoples) with its headquarters in Québec's Lower Town, had been one of the symposium's organizers.

But Jack Kerouac had been the spiritual father of the American beatnik movement and the English-speaking author of such books as the novel *On the Road.* His had been a voice of protest raised against the American consumer society of the 1950s. Was he now – almost twenty years after his death and with an unaccustomed accentuation of the first syllable of his name – to be made to serve the interests of Canada's French-speaking population?

Dussault was pleased to point out Kerouac's French-Canadian lineage as the descendant of eighteenth century Breton immigrants. As the son of poor parents, who during the Depression after the First World War had emigrated to the United States from the Rivière-du-Loup area on the St. Lawrence, he had grown up in the French quarter of Lowell, Massachusetts, and had spoken only French until he was six. Dussault said that the purpose of the Secretariat was to develop and promote a policy of *francophonie populaire* in North America.

This will be no easy task on a continent in which the English-speaking population has played a dominant role since the middle of the eighteenth century, and where today it constitutes a ninety-eight percent majority – all this despite the fact that large areas had been surveyed and (not least of all for the purposes of fur-trading) opened up by French explorers, missionaries and *coureurs de bois* (fur-traders). It was the French who explored the territory

...use on the ...Lawrence ...r between ...ntreal and ...ébec City. Typical of ...ébec is the richly ...namented balcony ...jecting out over the entrance.

850

Niagara Falls, North America's most spectacular natural phenomenon. The Canadian Falls are known as Horseshoe Falls.

surrounding the Great Lakes and the courses of the Mississipi, Missouri and Saskatchewan Rivers. They pushed forward from the St. Lawrence Lowlands, which had been the centre of New France, as far as the Rocky Mountains and the Gulf of Mexico. Their line of forts extended from Montreal to New Orleans. They prevented the British colonists of the Atlantic coast from crossing over the Appalachians into the interior of the continent – a significant grounds, in addition to rivalry in the fur trade, to square off the British against the French in North America. The conflict would finally come to an end in 1763, with France ceding the colonies that it had previously conquered by force of arms.

However, from that point on, the French subjects of the British Crown along the St. Lawrence – at that time numbering hardly more than 60,000 – would recognize only one aim in life: *la survivance*, survival while doing their utmost to preserve their cultural individuality. The remain to this day constantly aware of their French heritage. The heraldic legend on Québec's coat of arms *Je me souviens* ("I remember"), is to be read as an exhortation directed at today's Québec nationalists. As signs of their separateness French Canadians maintain strong ties with the Roman Catholic faith and French civil law (both permitted them by the apprehensive British on the eve of the American War of Independence as a means of discouraging the French from siding with the rebels). Similarly, they have persisted with their language, their rural way of life in which the village priest stands guard over convention and morality, the denominational school system and until the 1930s, employed a feudal system imported from France. Along with these tendencies, French-speaking families in the St. Lawrence Lowlands tended to become so blessed with children, that by 1837, their number had increased to half a million. *Revanche des berceaux* (the revenge of the cradles) was an elementary means of ensuring the survival of their cultural identity.

The ways in which this conflict between the Anglo-Saxon and French cultures has affected life in the decade leading up to World War II has been accurately depicted by Hugh MacLennan in his novel *Two Solitudes*, a classic of Canadian literature. It was, however, a conflict that in the 1970s and at the beginning of the 1980s was still threatening to tear Canada apart. The province of Québec, home to four out of five French-Canadians, appeared to be intent on political sovereignty and on seceding from the Canadian federation. Tens of thousands of English speakers left Québec for the neighbouring provinces,

driven away by rigorously applied language laws that, for instance, turned hot dogs and hamburgers into *chiens chauds* and *hambourgeois*, while department stores such as Eaton's and Steinberg's in Québec became obliged to dispense with the apostrophe in accordance with French grammatical rules.

While in 1980, the Québec population voted against seceding from Canada, two years later, the Government of Québec refused to grant approval to the repatriation of the Canadian Constitution; hitherto it was only the British North America Act, signed in London in 1867, that had served as Canada's constitution, with amendments having to be formally approved by the British Parliament. Now, the French-Canadians saw that various articles of the new Canadian Charter of Rights and Freedoms, above all those relating to linguistic minority rights, came into direct conflict with Québec's Charter of the French Language, which in the officially monolingual province granted absolute precedence to French in all spheres of official life.

Today it appears that the conflict has been resolved, for the present, at least at the government level. The Government of Québec finally added their approval to the Constitution after a clause was added expressly establishing Québec as a distinct society, a society with its own special character and a centre of francophonia in Canada. However, there are still a number of issues causing friction in everyday life. In Montreal, with its strong English-speaking minority, this is more evident than anywhere else in Québec. The year 1988 still saw English language signs and company names being painted over, display showcases kicked in, mass demonstrations of citizens fearful that the French language laws would be undermined, protests by the English-speaking population who felt constricted by the Charter of the French Language, as well as impassioned letters in the daily papers complaining, for example, that a railway conductor had spoken English.

A bee buzzing around a lion's nose, infuriating it but driving it into a corner, is how one cartoonist has chosen to describe Québec's relationship with the rest of Canada. It would not appear to be the most solid basis for relaxed relations between the two so-called founding nations, the British and the French. Nor is it conducive to a *francophonie populaire*.

When figures were published in 1988 showing a noticeably declining birth rate in Québec and with demographers already prophesizing the decline and fall of French culture in North America, the Toronto news-magazine Maclean's pulled no punches in

The imposing 100-metre-high Peace Tower stands watch over Parliament Buildings in the Canadian federal capital of Ottawa. The complex had to be rebuilt after a devastating fire in 1916.

Toronto and beyond can best be surveyed from atop the CN Tower, the tallest freestanding television tower in the world.

giving its report on this decline the title "The Revenge of the Cradles."

Fish and Beer

A warm and humid breeze was blowing over Great Slave Lake. It was early afternoon and the sun was high overhead. Our little island was bathed in warmth and enveloped in the scent wafting from stunted trees, decaying twigs and rank undergrowth.

We had spread out along the shore and were casting for fish. Klaus had suggested the trip and Greg and his friend had brought us out in their boat. We were now, perhaps some fifteen to twenty kilometres from Yellowknife. I had met Klaus, a Canadian from Germany, some years before in Québec. At that time, he had been working there for the government. Now he was the executive of an association in Yellowknife and travelled a lot in Canada's Northwest Territories. "In my job you need the saddle and bridle for a horse," he joked, "but what they've given me wouldn't be enough for a pony."

The light was reflecting off the water and turning it into a dazzling carpet. The lake was lapping peacefully on the shore. The island was a pile of rugged granite boulders almost one hundred metres across, with bright green-yellow lichens and small multicoloured flowers in the brushwood. There was a water-filled hollow in the centre of the island, surrounded by moss and a thicket of dead, bleached branches that crackled underfoot. Millennia of ice erosion had added their ripples to the flat shelf along the shoreline, giving it the structure of a washboard. Many generations must have passed before lichens had established themselves on this heap of rocks. Until mosses and grasses had followed them. Until dead plants had formed a layer of humus in which trees could take root. Apart from us, nobody was here.

I cast my line far and true. We roasted the trout that the others had caught. Klaus returned a little while later to the camp fire. A fish the size of a man's hand was swinging on his line, in which it had become utterly entangled. Klaus' trouser legs were wet. His line had jerked so unexpectedly that he had toppled over into the water. "You just leave a guy to drown," he grumbled. We ate the fish and bread and drank beer.

During the journey back, we spoke little. The sun had sunk low and the lake was growing dark. Maybe it was only because we were rather tired. But in this country one is frequently reduced to silence.

Greg sped up the boat to full speed and the bow rose out of the water. It was a fast boat. The wind was cool in our faces. The wake fanned out languidly for two or three hundered metres behind us. Beyond that the lake was calm. It was as though no one had ever been there.

TIMBERS AND TOWERS

Images of Canada in Narratives and Reports

The sheer vastness of Canada is of no doubt a major factor in the many cultural, historical and geographical contradictions which characterize it, and which are reflected in the various descriptions of Canada in the following pages. The diversity and ferocity of Canada's natural features present themselves in the hardship and alienation of prairie life as well as in the beauty and uniqueness of her people and landscape. While Canada rightly takes pride in her pluralistic society, she has often remained silent about her original residents, a silence now being broken by the natives themselves. Yet, such ambiguities are as unique and infinite as the impressions this seemingly boundless country offers the receptive traveller, not to mention the perceptive reader!

A Journey Through Canada

We left Kingston for Montreal on the tenth of May, at half-past nine in the morning, and proceeded in a steamboat down the St. Lawrence river. The beauty of this noble stream at almost any point, but especially in the commencement of this journey when it winds its way among the Thousand Islands, can hardly be imagined. The number and constant successions of these islands, all green and richly wooded; their fluctuating sizes, some so large that for half an hour together one among them will appear as the opposite

The unmistakable landmark of the CN Tower soars up 553 metres high into the sky over Toronto. The tower restaurant revolves slowly on its axis at a height of 400 metres. In the foreground, the Flat Iron Building.

bank of the river, and some so small that they are mere dimples on its broad bosom; their infinitve variety of shapes; and the numberless combinations of beautiful forms which the trees growing on them, present: all form a picture fraught with uncommon interest and pleasure. ...

The morning was ushered in by a violent thunderstorm, and was very wet, but gradually improved and brightened up. Going on deck after breakfast, I was amazed to see floating down with the stream, a most gigantic raft, with some thirty or forty wooden houses upon it, and at least as many flag masts, so that it looked like a nautical street. I saw many of these rafts afterwards, but never one so large. ...

At eight we landed again, and travelled by a stage-coach for four hours through a pleasant and well-cultivated country, perfectly French in every respect: in the appearance of the cottages; the air, language, and dress of the peasantry, the sign-boards on the shops and taverns; and the Virgin's shrines and crosses by the wayside. Nearly every common labourer and boy, though he had no shoes to his feet, wore round his waist a sash of some bright colour: generally red: and the women, who were working in the fields and gardens, and doing all kinds of husbandry, wore, one and all, great flat straw hats with most capacious brims. There were Catholic Priests and Sisters of Charity in the village streets; and images of the Saviour at the corners of cross-roads, and in other public places. ...

Montreal is pleasantly situated on the margin of the St. Lawrence, and is backed by some bold heights, about which there are charming rides and drives. The streets are generally narrow and irregular, as in most French towns of any age; but in the more modern parts of the city, they are wide and airy. They display a great variety of very good shops; and both in the town and suburbs there are many excellent private dwellings. The granite quays are remarkable for their beauty, solidity, and extent.

There is a very large Catholic cathedral here, recently erected; with two tall spires, of which one is yet unfinished. In the open space in front of this edifice, stands a solitary, grim-looking, square brick tower, which has a quaint and remarkable appearance, and which the wiseacres of the place have consequently determined to pull down immediately. The Government House is very superior to that at Kingston, and the town is full of life and bustle. ...

The impression made upon the visitor by this Gibraltar of America: its giddy heights; its citadel suspended, as it were, in the air; its picturesque steep streets and frowning gateways; and the splendid views which burst upon the eye at every turn: is at once unique and lasting.

The novelist CHARLES DICKENS (1812–1870) visited Canada in 1842. His particular talent for capturing both the unique and the ordinary is a feature of his observations of Canada.

Early Pioneer Memories

When we reached Hamburg, we paid what we still owed for the embarkation cards. We had no trouble getting to Quebec. When our train arrived in Winnipeg. I returned to Gretna. The Germans with whom I had become acquainted took me there and I found work with them.

I suppose that now you could call me a cowboy as I herded their cattle. Besides my regular wages I was given eighty bushels of wheat and forty bushels of barley. I stayed with the German families around Gretna for four years during which time I earned and saved a substantial amount of money. ...

It was time, I thought, to get some land for myself. These friendly Germans were very sorry to see me leave for, although I was of small build, I was a good worker.

I asked Windle, who owned a boxcar, to help me move. I loaded my two cows, two oxen, thirty hens, a wagon, a plow, twelve bags of flour, eight hams, and some cloth my wife had bought for the children. ... When I arrived at my brother's farm near Chipman, I discovered that he had already built a primitive shelter for me on my homestead. My first task was to build a permanent house, and I began to cut down trees for logs. I hauled them in during the day and at night I repaired the sleighs which I had made. However, my wife was strong and with her help we made steady progress. There was always so much hard work to do. The sun never saw me in bed for I was always up before sunrise. I was deep in debt when I bought a quarter section of land and then another one for my sons. I was always fond of cattle and I raised quite a few head. But then the prices dropped. A cow which used to be worth $140 had to be sold now for only eight dollars.

WASYL ELENIAK is officially recognized as being one of the first two Ukrainians to arrive in Canada,

31

in 1891. He received his Canadian citizenship in January 1947 at the first ceremony to be held in Canada. This passage is taken from a recording of his memoirs, done during a 1940 visit to the Basilian Father's Monastery in Mundare, Alberta.

From Femme to Fairhaven

The Island of Newfoundland is justly famous for place names with a punch. Famished Gut is an example. And Rogue's Harbour. There are also Horse Chops and Hole-in-the-Wall, not to mention Sally's Leg and Virgin's Arm, all named in the distant past by sailors and fishermen with a sense of humour.

But the Post Office Department is doing its best to abolish these salty place names and to substitute such masterpieces as Port Elizabeth and Fairhaven. ... We Newfoundlanders are all in favour of these improvements. We do not want to live in Hole-in-the-Wall. We want to live in Parkdale. It sounds so nice and sanitary.

We feel that if the Canada Post Office succeeds in getting rid of all the old place names we will be much the better for it. We are even prepared to help them out by supplying them with a list of old names that they've never heard of yet. At least, we are pretty certain that they have never heard of them, since they have never managed to deliver any mail there. Devil's Thumb, for instance. I'll bet they've never delivered a letter to Devil's Thumb in all their born days.

And then there's Fom. That isn't really the way you spell it. On the map it is spelled "Femme", but everyone who lives there calls it Fom, so Fom it must be. There's a story about Fom:

An American yacht with a fishing party was plying along the northern inlets of Fortune Bay one evening, and tied up to a stage head in a small cove. This island offshore was known as Petticoat Island, but the Americans didn't know that. The yachting skipper accosted the first baccy-chewing character he met on the stage.

"Hello," he greeted. "Where are we? What do you call this settlement?"

"Fom," said the baccy-chewer, casting a speculative eye at the weather.

"OK," said the American. "We want to send a message home. Where's the telegraph office?"

"Fifteen miles out the bay," said the native, adding that they usually rowed there in a dory.

"Post office?" said the American hopefully.

"One over in English Harbour East," the fisherman explained. "Ye must've passed it comin' along shore."

"No telegraph, no post office, no roads!" the American exclaimed. "Do you have radios here?"

"Well," the fisherman drawled, "they's a couple. But we don't turn 'em on much. Can't get the stations up in St. John's, and them Canadian fellers never seems to have any news worth while."

"Well!" exclaimed the American. "You people in Fom are really cut off from the world, aren't you?"

"S'pose so," said the fisherman.

"Why," continued the yacht skipper, "if New York burned down tonight you wouldn't know anything about it!"

"That's true, I s'pose," the fisherman admitted, "but then," – and he paused to squirt a philosophic stream of baccy juice over the stage head – "if Fom burned down you fellers up in New York wouldn't know anything about it, either!"

HAROLD HARWOOD (b. 1923) was a member of the Newfoundland legislature between 1949 and 1951. He has continued to criticize the wanton destruction of Canada's heritage and environment which is carried out in the name of "progress" by the Canadian authorities.

Adopting a Culture

That camping trip to Sam Ford Fiord was a turning point in my life. I had been north on several brief occasions before, but had never had the opportunity to be immersed in the real life of the Inuit. Camp life is where language, tradition, housekeeping (or tentkeeping) and hunting all come together. It was all so new and wonderful to me – icebergs, sea animals, meals of fresh meat cooked over a heather fire, the men packing caribou carcasses back to camp, children playing out hunting episodes and climbing over the rocks, delicate flowers and glacial scree, fresh cold water to drink and, all around, mountains cradling glaciers and reaching to the sky from the ice-decorated waters of the ocean. Little did I know then how commonplace these things – and this family – would become for me.

I had no notion of taking on a new culture when I came to Clyde River. I took my camera everywhere in those first two months, a curious bystander, one who would take some language, memories and hundreds of photographs back to show the folks at home. Indeed, I naively thought that I could drop in for a year, learn Inuktitut and then leave again to pick up my southern lifestyle. But the process of learning Inuktitut requires that one immerse oneself in the land and the sea and the sky, in the stories of the elders and in the life of a close-knit community. If

southern Ontario, a dominantly agricultural region, there are many such typical farmyards.

Pasturelands along the Saskatchewan River. Here lie the last untouched prairie grasslands of North America.

Jasper [Nati]onal Park [on t]he border between [Al]berta and British Columbia offers [p]rimordial scenes of [m]ountains [ ] untouched [me]adowland [ ] the foot of [th]e Rockies.

Banff National Park, founded in 1885, was the first such park to be established in Canada. Here the view is of the Main Ranges.

Prairie Country

Saskatchewan, you always seem to me
A women without favour in your face,
Flat-breasted, angular, devoid of grace.
Why do men woo you? naught is fair to see
In that wide visage with thin unkempt hair,
And form that squarely stands, feet splayed apart.

The lines express what is in fact a common misconception; the truth is that the Saskatchewan landscape is never barren (except in times of prolonged drought) and in few places flat. The great southern plains are seamed deep by gullies and creek beds and frequently ridged by low hills which at a distance appear bathed in a romantic blue-green haze; two hundred miles north of the border the plains merge into pleasant, rolling parkland which in turn yields after another two hundred miles or more to a vast forest-lake-and-muskeg belt impinging on the subarctic terrain of the barren lands. And everywhere there are things to be seen and felt that exalt or soothe the sensitive spirit: crocuses spreading a mauve mist along railway embankments before the last patch of dirty grey snow has melted; wheatfields merging into a wave-surfaced green or golden ocean, unbounded save for an incredibly remote horizon rim at times indistinguishable from the sky itself; autumn days when the wind is miraculously quiet and premonitions of winter-death impel a man to look on a landscape of muted greys and browns with the passionate intensity of a lower parting from his beloved; mid-winter hoar-frost hanging on fence and telephone wires like strung popcorn; and the occasional vista – from the top of a ridge or butte or even a grain elevator – when a man sees all the kingdoms of the earth stretched out at his feet and feels himself a creature of utter insignificance in the sum of things or else the very centre of the universe. ...

Nowhere else in the west does the stranger feel himself more explosed to the wrath of the gods and the fury of the elements than in the middle of the Saskatchewan prairie.

Even though he may be sheltered behind walls. A sign in each unit of a Maple Creek motel reads thus: When the wind blows please hang on to the door...

EDWARD McCOURT (1907 – 1972) was born in Ireland and emigrated to Canada in 1909. His novels are set on the Canadian prairies and focus on the critical struggle between the dream and reality in which his characters are caught.

Lost in Time and Space

Was it only yesterday that men sailed around the moon ... And can they now stand up on its barren surface? You and I marvel that man should travel so far and so fast ... Yet, if they have travelled far then I have travelled farther ... and if they have travelled fast, then I faster ... for I was born a thousand years ago ... born in a culture of bows and arrows. But within the span of half a lifetime I was flung across the ages to the culture of the atom bomb ... And from bows and arrows to atom bombs is a distance far beyond a flight to the moon.

I was born in an age that loved the things of nature and gave them beautiful names like Tes-wall-u-wit instead of dried-up names like Stanley Park.

I was born when people loved all nature and spoke to it as though it had a soul ... I can remember going up Indian River with my father when I was very young ... I can remember him watching the sun light fires on Mount Pay-nay-nay as it rose above its peak. I can remember him singing his thanks to it as he often did ... singing the Indian word "thanks ..." so very, very softly.

And then the people came ... more and more people came ... like a crushing rushing wave they came ... hurling the years aside!! and suddenly I found myself a young man in the midst of the twentieth century.

I found myself and my people adrift in this new age ... but not a part of it.

Engulfed by its rushing tide, but only as a captive eddy ... goin round and round ... On little reserves, on plots of land we floated in a kind of grey unreality ... ashamed of our culture which you ridiculed ... unsure of who we were or where we were going ... uncertain of our grip on the present ... weak in our hope of the future ... And that is pretty well where we stand today.

I had a glimpse of something better than this. For a few brief years I knew my people when we lived the old life ... I knew them when there was still a dignity in our lives and a feeling of worth in our outlook. I knew them when there was unspoken confidence in the home and a certain knowledge of the path we walked upon. But we were living on the dying energy of a dying culture ... a culture that was slowly losing its forward thrust.

I think it was the suddenness of it all that hurt us so. We did not have time to adjust to the startling upheaval around us. We seemed to have lost what we had without a replacement for it. We did not have time to take our twentieth-century progress and eat it

Owing to its fjord-like setting in Burrard Inlet, Vancouver Harbour is one of the largest natural harbours in the world. Nowadays, it is a major airport and port centre.

43

Long Beach in Pacific Rim National Park on Vancouver Island.

little by little and digest it. It was forced feeding from the start and our stomachs turned sick and we vomited.

CHIEF DAN GEORGE is a well-known contemporary Indian writer. His essay My Very Good Dear Friends *marked the beginning of writing by the Canadian Indians, a new force in Canadian literature.*

A Winter Wonderland

It has been a long, brutal winter. And it has barely started.

After the cold, the snow, the blizzards and the wind, we're all fed up with the cruelest season. But there is a silver lining. It's frozen, like everything else, but it's there.

We've had a bit of everything (except warm air, that is) in Edmonton this winter. We've had a blinding blizzard. We've had – 30 degree temperatures. We've had windchill that could freeze your flesh in minutes. Of course, we're griping and complaining, swaping horror stories about balky cars and frozen fingers and iced over windows. Old timers – if 1969 can be considered old – will remember the great freeze of Jan. 7 to Feb. 1 of that year, when the temperature never rose above zero Fahrenheit.

Edmonton is defined by its climate. More than the world's largest shopping mall, or the world's best hockey team, weather makes Edmonton what it is. We seem almost embarrassed by it, but we shouldn't be. It's a badge of honor, really. After all, how many cities of more than half a million souls can operate fairly normally in minus 30 degree weather? Would New Yorkers get to work on time? Would Torontonians keep their schools open? Would Vancouverites shop and dine and go about their daily lives? No, no and no.

We have nothing to be ashamed of. We've built a big, strong, vibrant city in an inhospitable climate. We should be proud, Frozen, but proud.

And if that doesn't do it, spring is only 67 days away.

This editorial appeared in the Edmonton Examiner, *13 January 1991; it was accompanied by a cartoon captioned "What's blue, numb, – 30° C, and white all over? Edmonton!" Though the city annually endures a coldspell, the temperature on 15 January 1991 was + 4° C, and on 17 January, + 10° C.*

...and a 4,500-kilometre-*ong ribbon of asphalt connects Alert, the thernmost ettlement, with ndsor, the thernmost Canadian cities.*

CANADA
CONCISE TRAVEL GUIDE

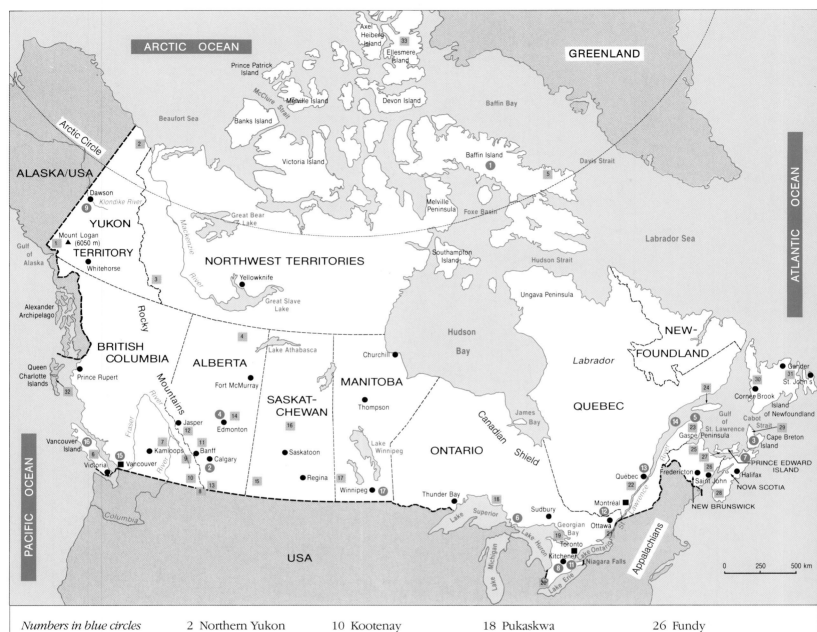

Numbers in blue circles refer to places mentioned in the travel guide.

Numbers in green squares refer to **Canadian National Parks:**

1 Kluane

2 Northern Yukon	10 Kootenay
3 Nahanni	11 Banff
4 Wood Buffalo	12 Jasper
5 Auyuittuq	13 Waterton Lakes
6 Pacific Rim	14 Elk Island
7 Mount Revelstoke	15 Grasslands
8 Glacier	16 Prince Albert
9 Yoho	17 Riding Mountain

18 Pukaskwa	26 Fundy
19 Georgian Bay Islands	27 Prince Edward Island
20 Point Pelee	28 Kejimkujik
21 Saint Lawrence Islands	29 Cape Breton Highlands
22 La Mauricie	30 Gros Morne
23 Forillon	31 Terra Nova
24 Mingan Archipelago	32 South Moresby
25 Kouchibouguac	33 Ellesmere Island

TOURIST INFORMATION

The first place to turn to for visitors to Canada is the tourist section at Canada House, Trafalgar Square, Cockspur Street, London SW1Y 5BJ, tel. (71) 6 29 94 92, or at the Canadian Embassy, 501 Pennsylvania Avenue, N.W., Washington, D.C. 20001, tel. (202) 6 82-17 40.
Within Canada itself, maps and many other information materials are readily available. Visitor Centres, indicated by a bold question mark sign, are situated in most cities and towns, on the provincial borders and in all national parks.

GENERAL INFORMATION

BEARS. Black bears, grizzlies and polar bears are all to be found in Canada and one does not have to look long. The small black bears (which also can be brown) are to be encountered in every region. Perhaps you will see this omnivore not far out of town running across the road or scavenging in garbage dumps. On the other hand, the habitat of the reclusive grizzly is the Rocky Mountains and the Arctic tundra. Polar bears, which can weigh up to seven hundred kilograms, are constantly on the move along the ice pack of the far north and along the coastline of the Arctic Ocean. So it is with the black bear that unwary visitors are most likely to come into contact: for example, if campers keep food in their tents overnight (best hang it up in a tree!), when unwashed crockery gives off an inviting aroma, or when hikers pass through the wilderness downwind of a bear (best noisily announce your approach!). So, keep your distance and observe the "bear regulations" displayed in the national and provincial parks.

FISHING. Canada is a genuine paradise for anglers: Ontario alone has over 400,000 lakes, and throughout the country, visitors will find hunting and fishing lodges, many of them more than comfortably equipped. But even beginners who wish to fish in streams and lakes will encounter no problems; a permit costs between ten and thirty dollars, depending on the province. Proof of proficiency is not required and restrictive regulations are rare. (Only salmon, being much in demand, are safeguarded by strict regulations.)

LANGUAGE. Since 1969, both English and French have been recognized as Canada's official languages. Eighty-five percent of the almost seven million French-speaking Canadians – after the English-Canadians the largest and most culturally conscious segment of the country's population – live in Québec. Additionally, there are large German, Italian, Ukrainian, Chinese, East Indian and Polish groups that are slowly becoming assimilated. Except for a few remote localities in Québec, the visitor will find English spoken everywhere.

MOSQUITOES. From June until the middle of August, visitors to Canada are prone to be plagued by these insistent little creatures, which appear often in gigantic swarms by lakes and in forests. While European repellents may simply attract them, Canadian ones often prove

At Blue Rocks in the Canadian maritime province of Nova Scotia.

Canada at a Glance	Area (km²)	Inhabitants	Inhabitants per km²	Accession to the Canadian Federation	Capital
Alberta	661,190	2,386,000	3.6	1905	Edmonton
British Columbia	947,800	2,926,000	3.1	1871	Victoria
Manitoba	649,950	1,083,000	1.7	1870	Winnipeg
New Brunswick	73,440	721,000	9.8	1867	Fredericton
Newfoundland	405,720	580,000	1.6	1949	Saint John's
Nova Scotia	55,490	888,000	16.0	1867	Halifax
Ontario	1,068,580	9,273,000	8.7	1867	Toronto
Prince Edward Island	5,660	128,000	22.6	1873	Charlottetown
Québec	1,540,000	6,658,000	4.3	1867	Québec
Saskatchewan	652,330	1,022,000	1.6	1905	Regina
Northwest Terr.	3,426,320	50,000	0.01	–	Yellowknife
Yukon Territory	483,450	24,000	0.05	–	Whitehorse
Canada	9,970,610	25,738,000	2.5		Ottawa

somewhat more effective. It's a small consolation to know that, though a pesky irritation, they don't spread disease.

ROYAL CANADIAN MOUNTED POLICE, Canada's federal police are famed not least of all for their red coats and were indeed formerly mounted. Today's Mounties, at least 20,000 strong, were established more than a century ago as the Northwest Mounted Police to bring law and order to the wild west. They continue to operate as a police force in the north and in smaller

townships throughout the country. At their training headquarters in Regina, Saskatchewan, recruits can be watched being put through their paces, and the museum displays commemorate the force's finest hours.

INDUSTRY AND TRADE

HUDSON'S BAY COMPANY. On 2 May 1670, Britain's Prince Rupert – together with London businessmen – founded one of the largest commercial empires in history: the Hudson's Bay Company. It was primarily fur traders working for this company that opened up western and northern Canada in their search for beaver pelts, whereby they set up a network of trading posts across the territory. The area belonging to the company, Rupert's Land, comprised almost four million square kilometres. After being sold to the Dominion of Canada in 1869, the company remained in the fur trade and developed into a large chain of department stores, which still operate today.

The LUMBER INDUSTRY. The lumberjack, with his loud red and black checkered shirt and ribald humour, has become a symbol of Canada – and justly

The Péribonca River, Québec.

In the Holland Marsh District of Ontario, vegetables are cultivated in vast fields.

so: one in every ten jobs is connected with the lumber industry. Forty-four percent of the country is covered by forest and 150 million cubic metres of timber are felled annually. Canadian timber is made into pulp to provide newsprint for one-third of the newspapers produced around the world, be it in Japan or Europe.

OIL. The first oil strike was in Turner Valley, south of Calgary, in 1914. Ever since, the wells of the western prairies have not stopped gushing and annual production levels have meanwhile reached the value of some ten billion dollars. The "black gold" has turned the

oil centres of Calgary and Edmonton into boom towns over the course of the past few decades. In northern Alberta, near Fort McMurray, gigantic oil reserves, amounting possibly to 600 billion barrels, have been located in tar sand deposits which are now to be exploited by means of innovative mining techniques.

WHEAT is cultivated on close to fifteen million hectares and, earning over four billion dollars annually, ranks as the country's most important agricultural export. The plains of the prairie provinces of Saskatchewan and Alberta, with their dry, hot climate and fertile

soil which makes them ideally suited to wheat production, are often described as the breadbasket of Canada. From here the grain is shipped all over the world via the port of Churchill on the Hudson Bay and via the St. Lawrence River.

ORIGINAL RESIDENTS

The ESKIMOS, see under "Inuit".

The INDIANS. Before the white man appeared, a variety of Indian cultures existed in Canada, ranging from the Algonquin and the warlike Iroquois in the east to the West Coast tribes famous for their carved totem poles. However, diseases brought in from Europe drastically reduced the native population. Nowadays, there are again some 400,000 Indians; they live on numerous small reservations in almost six hundred different tribal groups scattered throughout the country. In shops on the reservations, visitors can often purchase beautiful carvings and bead and braid work, and so help to alleviate the original inhabitants' lot in the face of high unemployment and a low standard of living.

Totem poles, which nowadays are to be found made of plastic in every souvenir shop and which are intended to symbolized the Indian culture, properly belong only in the cultural sphere of the Pacific Coast tribes. For the Kwakiutl, Nootka and Tlingit, they stood for centuries as symbols of the power and wealth of individual tribes. Missionaries prohibited these supposedly graven images during the last century and it has only been in recent years that the Indian's versatile craftsmanship as wood carvers has experienced a renaissance. The finest examples of both old and new totem poles can be seen in the Museum of Anthropology at the University of British Columbia in Vancouver and in the Royal British Columbia Museum in Victoria.

INUIT means "human beings" and is what the original inhabitants of Canada's Arctic call themselves. It was the neighbouring Indian tribes that labelled them "Eskimos", namely raw meat eaters. Today some 26,000 Inuit, whose ancestors migrated from Alaska about 1,000 years ago, live in Canada.

The majority are settled in widely dispersed Arctic Ocean communities. However, their traditional way of life as hunters is nowadays being increasingly affected as it comes under the influence of a highly mechanized "white" civilization. Some villages, for example Baker Lake and Cape Dorset, have specialized in sculptures especially of soap stone and prints, which are greatly treasured by galleries in southern Canada.

The MÉTIS. The descendants of Indian women and early French fur traders constitute the third ethnic group of Canada's original inhabitants – after the Indians and Inuit. The Métis, today numbering some 100,000, are a predominantly French-speaking minority. As fur traders and early settlers, they made an important contribution to opening up the continent. However, nowadays they are somewhat forgotten. Most live in the north of the prairie provinces, where they often lead an impoverished existence as trappers or in cultivating smallholdings.

TRANSPORT

CANOEING. Owing to Canada's innumerable waterways, the Indian invention of the canoe provides the best means of transport through the pathless wilderness. Up until the present day, the country has remained an eldorado for adventurous canoeists. Canoes can be rented for a reasonable hire charge everywhere and there is sure to be a practice stretch nearby. Novices who are eager to re-evoke a trapper's existence will find attractive routes in Algonquin Provincial Park in Ontario or in La Maurice National Park in Québec; the more proficient paddler can accept the challenge offered by northern rivers and streams, the Nahanni River or in Quetico Provincial Park.

ROADS THROUGH THE WILDER-NESS. Anyone who wishes to get really close to nature will find that the boundless forests of Canada offer ideal opportunities for camping and fishing, far off the beaten track. Dempster Highway, stretching for 720 kilometres from Dawson City to Inuvik on the Mackenzie Delta, is regarded as the loneliest and wildest itinerary that the north has to offer. But other routes in the Northwest Territories, in the Yukon and in the northern regions of all the prairie provinces also lead the visitor for the most part through untouched wilderness.

Any driver who uses these remote gravel roads will require good maps and such additional equipment as extra spare tyres and fuel, a protective grill for the windscreen, emergency rations and mosquito repellents.

TRANS-CANADA HIGHWAY. The famous transcontinental highway from the Atlantic to the Pacific, the first road to traverse the entire country, was completed in 1962 at Rogers Pass in the Rocky Mountain.

The asphalt ribbon threads its way over 7,821 kilometres from St. John's in Newfoundland to Victoria, British Columbia on the Pacific. The two termini, both situated on islands, are each reached via ferry.

It is particularly the scenic beauties of the stretches along the St. Lawrence River and through the Rocky Mountains that make this a journey well worth undertaking.

ANNUAL EVENTS AND FESTIVALS

The enthusiasm for life manifested by Canadians is infectious – be it at the numerous celebrations held by ethnic groups and professions, at local music festivals, or at the pioneer days commemorated in smaller communities. There is always something happening: an Indian pow-wow or a rodeo, a lobster festival in a fishing village, or the colourful parades organized by local pioneer clubs. While visitor centres will provide details of local festivities, listed below is just a small selection of the better-known events:

Canadians like to celebrate out in the open – even during the bitterly cold winter months. In the middle of February, Catholic Québec celebrates Carnival as ten days of pre-lenten frivolity that includes a perilous rowing competition on the partially frozen St. Lawrence River. Meanwhile in Ottawa, the federal capital enjoys Winterlude and takes to the frozen Rideau Canal for skating and the annual ice sculpture competition, while in The Pas lumberjacks meet up for the Northern Manitoba Trapper Festival.

In April in Québec villages, spring is welcomed at parties where the freshly-tapped maple syrup plays a central role. The Festival of Spring, celebrated in Ottawa in May, sees millions of tulips blossoming around the halls in which concerts and theatrical performances take place. On Victoria Day, at the end of May, parades are held throughout the country celebrating the British heritage, Victoria holds its large Swiftsure Sailing Regatta and in Montreal, it's time to begin the International Fireworks Days' competitions.

Summertime in the west of the country means logging festivals, rodeos and Indian pow-wows. At the end of June, Montreal has its International Jazz Festival, and at the end of July, Toronto pulsates to Caribbean rhythms during Caribana, a West Indies carnival. The entire summer months are devoted to large theatre festivals in Charlottetown, Stratford (Shakespeare, of course) and Niagara-on-the-Lake (Shaw). Québec's Festival d'Eté offers music and French Canadian folklore.

Canada's national holiday on 1 July is celebrated throughout the land with parades and "birthday parties". Immediately afterwards, Calgary gives itself over to the ten-day frenzy of the Calgary Stampede, the largest rodeo in the world.

In the middle of August, it's time for gold prospectors on the Klondike to gather in Dawson City to drink a toast or two – or more – in honour of Discovery Days. September is marked by harvest and thanksgiving celebrations, and in the east, by wine festivals.

FOOD AND DRINK

Canadian cuisine reflects the many and varied preferences and recipes that immigrants have brought with them. The first settlers, the French and the British, continued the gastronomic traditions of their mother countries, while adopting from the Indians a number of hitherto unknown ingredients, such as corn, pumpkin and the vitamin-rich maple syrup that nowadays is served with the typical breakfast pancake.

In Québec, French Canadian cooking has continued to develop over the centuries and has long since come to be regarded as providing the best cuisine available in the country. Since later immigrants brought with them their varied culinary traditions, one may well be tempted along a single street by Chinese chop suey, Russian pirogi, Jewish latkes and tender steak from Alberta. Before becoming too surfeited to enjoy anything more, one should at least be sure to try the sweet and typically Canadian blueberry pie.

Particularly in country districts – in cafés and small restaurants – the food is as appetizing and the portions are as generous as any hungry hiker or angler could ever wish.

Many local restaurants specialize in lighter, more refined cuisine and here, particularly, Canadian fish and lobster is to be recommended. Wild game, however, does not appear on restaurant menues since Canadian hunters serve it only in their homes (sale is prohibited).

PLACES OF INTEREST

Circled numbers refer to the map; italicized numbers refer to the colour photographs.

The ARCTIC. Approximately one-quarter of Canada's land surface lies north of the tree line, which swings in a wide arc from the mouth of the Mackenzie River in the west to the southern point of the Hudson Bay. The northern part of the region includes a vast group of islands, the Arctic Archipelago, which is enclosed in pack ice for the entire winter half of the year. However, it is not merely a land of ice and snow. Only the mountains in the east and the north are perpetually buried beneath glaciers: the broad tundra regions west of the Hudson Bay turn green during the short summer and in September are resplendent in autumnal hues. This is the habitat of foxes and blue hares, of countless water fowl and of the rare musk ox. Only some 20,000 people, predominantly Inuit, live in tiny communities along the Arctic Ocean coastline, without roads connecting them with the outside world.

lobster dishes served in the restaurants of picturesque fishing villages.

BAFFIN ISLAND ①. With a surface area totalling 507,451 square kilometres, this island in the eastern Arctic Ocean is Canada's largest and the fifth largest in the world. The western part of this treeless island is characterized by vast tundra plains that stretch to the Arctic Circle, while rugged mountains tower over the interior and along the east coast, beside Baffin Bay. The mighty glaciers of the Penny Ice Cap, a remnant of the last ice age, inch their way down from the over two thousand-metre-high mountains of Auyuittuq National Park. Noteworthy among the few settlements

The Grand Falls, New Brunswick.

The ATLANTIC COAST. Newfoundland, Nova Scotia, New Brunswick and Prince Edward Island are the easternmost of Canada's provinces, and have the longest history of settlement. Nevertheless, their interiors have, for the most part, remained densely forested. The agriculture industry dominates only on the sickle-shaped Prince Edward Island, where the red soil is ideal for potato cultivation. Tourists will come to appreciate the deserted bays and the long sandy beaches around the Gulf of St. Lawrence – and as well, the exquisite

is the artistic colony of Cape Dorset, where Inuit craftsmen produce prints and sculptures.

CALGARY ②. The city of the famous Calgary Stampede, the largest rodeo in the world (also see under "Festivals") and the host of the 1988 Olympic Winter Games, was founded as recently as 1875 as a fort for the Northwest Mounted Police in the days of the wild west. The westward expansion of the railway in 1883 and the discovery of oil in this century have provided the

The coastal region of Ne[w] Brunswick in eastern Canada.

impetus to turn this formerly sleepy one-horse town in Alberta into a modern oil metropolis. Of special interest are the Glenbow Museum, which displays the history of the Canadian West, and the Calgary Tower, which offers a panoramic view, across the prairies, as far as the Rocky Mountains. *36, 37*

The CANADIAN SHIELD. Canada's largest geological formation lies around the Hudson Bay like a horseshoe. Its Pre-Cambrian rock counts among the oldest of the earth's formations. It is especially apparent in northern Ontario how ice age glaciers shaped the Shield: mountains were eroded away to become flat granite domes between

Legislative Building in Edmonton.

The Old Town Clock in Halifax.

which innumerable lakes gleam and glisten. The rock, some even as old as 3.6 billion years, is rich in minerals. In the northern reaches of the provinces of Québec, Ontario and Manitoba, gold, silver, zinc, nickel, cobalt and uranium are mined.

CAPE BRETON ISLAND ③. This island, east of Nova Scotia with 10,300 square kilometres, was one of the first areas of settlement in North America. Here, Scotish settlers built their homes along a rugged coastline washed by the

surging sea; indeed, Gaelic is still spoken in a few remote villages. Of particular interest is the elaborately detailed reconstruction of the French fortress of Louisbourg and the panoramic drive of Cabot Trail, which leads around the northeastern tip of the island.

EDMONTON ④. Alberta's capital on the northern edge of the prairies lies in the middle of a productive oil field and is the gateway to the mineral wealth of the Canadian north. The most recent

attraction in this modern city is West Edmonton Mall combining a large covered recreational facility with the world's largest shopping mall – including five hundred shops, an aquarium, hotel and a swimming pool with artificially induced waves.

GASPÉ (Gaspésie) ⑤. This rocky peninsula on the south bank of the St. Lawrence estuary in Québec provides some of eastern Canada's most lovely scenery. The steep cliffs of Forillon National Park and the famous red rocks of the small town of Percé number among the scenic splendours of a coast indented by many bays. *6/7*

The GREAT LAKES ⑥. An enormous lowland area, which came into being during the last ice age, contains the five lakes of Ontario, Erie, Huron, Michigan and Superior. Their 246,000 square kilometres constitute the largest fresh water area in the world (approximately the size of Great Britain). Lake Michigan is entirely within the United States, while only the northern halves of the other four are part of Canadian territory. Lake Ontario's shoreline is densely populated, located in Canada's economic centre. Further to the north, Lake Huron's warm waters and Lake Superior's limpid depths are bordered by lonely woodlands. Much of the lakeside shore is protected national and provincial parkland that beckons canoeists, swimmers and yachtsmen.

HALIFAX ⑦. Since its foundation as a military port in 1749, it has been soldiers and seafarers who have determined the charter of the largest Canadian port on the Atlantic. Its imposing citadel, built in 1828 above the harbour, has never had to withstand attack and is now a military museum. The surroundings are most attractive, particularly Nova Scotia's rugged south coast with such picturesque fishing villages as Peggy's Cove.

KITCHENER ⑧, one hundred kilometres west of Toronto, was founded by the Mennonites around 1800. During the nineteenth century, it became the most important settlement for Germans in Canada and up until the First World War was named Berlin.

Many traditions have been kept up until the present: the restaurants offer German cooking, German-style sausage and bread is on sale at the Farmer's Market, and in autumn there is a large Oktoberfest. In the surrounding area, the Mennonites keep up their traditional, deeply religious way of life.

The KLONDIKE ⑨. In August 1896, prospectors discovered rich deposits of gold along the Klondike River, a small tributary of the Yukon River, near the Alaska border. When – months later – reports reached the outside world, it started the biggest gold rush in history. "To the Klondike!" was the cry that echoed from London to San Francisco. Dawson City mushroomed overnight and soon numbered 30,000 residents. However, when the boom had ended a few years later, Dawson City turned into a ghost town. Only in recent years has the tourist industry brought business back into this wilderness.

MONTREAL ⑩, one of Canada's cultural and economic centres, has close to three million residents, making it, after Paris, the largest French-speaking city in the world. The metropolis is situated on an island of the same name in the St. Lawrence River. The churches and merchants' houses of the old town crowd together along the river bank, behind which, at the foot of Mount Royal, are the towering skyscrapers of the highly modern inner city. Its cosmopolitan atmosphere and *joie de vivre* is characterized by a pulsating night life, street cafés, good restaurants and boutiques on Rue Sainte-Catherine and Rue Saint-Denis, a lively theatre season and numerous cultural festivals. Small holiday resorts and scenic, hiking paths in Québec's provincial Parc des Laurentides encourage visitors to make day excursions into the surrounding area. *19*

NATIONAL PARKS. "Take nothing but photographs, leave nothing but footprints" – this is the National Parks' code of conduct. Since the first protected area Banff National Park, was founded in 1885, Canada's system of national parks now numbers over thirty and covers some 180,000 square kilometres. And districts continue to be considered for park status. They include a variety of ecosystems and the most beautiful scenery, ranging from the rugged coastline along the Pacific Rim or in Gros Morne National Park to the grandiose high mountain parks of Banff, Jasper, Kootenay and Yoho and the deserted tundra landscapes of Ellesmere Island and Baffin Island in the Arctic. The underlying intention is to maintain the pristine wilderness for future generations to enjoy. Therefore, luxury is not what is offered but rather splendid camping sites, hiking trails and panoramic drives (see map on page 48 for the location of individual national parks).

NIAGARA FALLS ⑪. Every year, the most famous natural wonder of North America casts its spell over twelve million visitors. Here, the foaming waters of the Niagara River, which connect Lake Erie and Lake Ontario, plunge fifty-five metres down into the gorge that the river has hollowed out during the last 12,000 years – at a rate of 150 million litres of water every minute. While the border between the United States and Canada is indeed in the middle of the river, ninety percent of the water cascades over the more impressive Canadian falls, Horseshoe Falls. *22/23*

OTTAWA ⑫. In 1853, Queen Victoria proclaimed a remote logging camp on the Ottawa River as the new capital of the united Canadian colonies, much to the amazement at that time of many Canadians. That rough and rugged camp has meanwhile been transformed into a trim administrative centre with its neo-Gothic parliament buildings, carefully tended parks along the water's edge and numerous excellent museums. Of particular interest is the new Museum of Civilization, located across the Ottawa River, with its comprehensive ethnological exhibitions devoted to Canada's original inhabitants. *25*

The PRAIRIES. The broad and unending plains between the Rocky Mountains and the forests of Ontario were originally grasslands, home to large buffalo herds and their hunters, the Assiniboine and Blackfoot Indians. Following the construction of the railway in 1885, white settlers began to farm the fertile land, its soil deposited by ice age lakes. The former prairie grass survives nowadays only in a few protected areas and has been replaced by golden fields of waving wheat reaching to the horizon. The prairies are commonly known as the "breadbasket of Canada". The principal settlements are situated along the Saskatchewan and

Hull on the Ottawa River which has meanwhile grown to meet with Ottawa

Red Rivers, which flow out into the Hudson Bay. *2, 34/35*

QUÉBEC ⑬. The capital of the French-speaking province of the same name is perched above the St. Lawrence River atop a 110-metre-high cliff. Winding alleyways in the old town centre, the encompassing town walls still intact and the luxurious Hôtel Château Frontenac looming high above endow this city, founded by the explorer Samuel de Champlain in 1608, with an almost medieval appearance – to the delight of the numerous American tourists. The surrounding area is also worth visiting including the well-maintained age old villages on the Île Sainte-Hélène, the eighty-three metre-high Montmorency Waterfall and Sainte-Anne-de-Beaupré, a

the wide variety of flora and fauna have made the Rockies a popular tourist attraction. Five national parks, including the high mountain parks of Banff and Jasper, as well as a number of provincial parks safeguard the unique mountain scenery. Doubtlessly the most beautiful – and most frequented – route in the Rocky Mountains is Highway 93, the Icefields Parkway between Lake Louise and Jasper.

ST. LAWRENCE RIVER ⑭. The river that has become an integral part of Canada's history flows from the Great Lakes into the Atlantic. It was along this river that explorers and fur traders penetrated into the interior of the country, and it was along its banks that the first white settlements came into

TORONTO ⑪. Situated on the shore of Lake Ontario, with its more than three million inhabitants, Toronto is the largest city as well as the financially and industrially most important one in Canada. Although not founded until 1793 and for a long time disparaged as "boringly British", Ontario's capital has been greatly changed by all the immigrants who have arrived since World War II. Excellent museums and art galleries, exemplary skyscraper architecture and a flourishing cultural life (the National Ballet of Canada and the Toronto Symphony Orchestra) help to determine the city's presentday character. A particular attraction is the 553-metre-high CN Tower, the tallest freestanding television tower in the world. From the viewing platform, one

On the St. Lawrence River.

pilgrimage destination on the north bank of the river. *14/15, 17, 18*

The ROCKY MOUNTAINS. The largest mountain chain of the North American Cordilleras extends in Canada from the US border for some 1,200 kilometres northwards. During the last ice age, glaciers determined the present shape of the slate, lime and sandstone mountains that came into existence during the Tertiary Period. Snow-covered mountain peaks and deep gorges, shimmering mountain lakes and

existence. Fifteen million people, almost two-thirds of all Canadians, now live in the St. Lawrence Lowlands between Windsor and Québec. Its presentday significance as the continent's most important waterway dates from 1959 when the St. Lawrence Seaway was completed.

During the summer season, a system of locks enables large cargo ships to sail in from the Atlantic for over 3,700 kilometres deep into the heart of the country as far as Thunder Bay on Lake Superior. *4/5*

looks out over the tops of all the buildings as far as the distant horizon. The mood after the sun has set is particularly memorable. *26/27, 29*

VANCOUVER ⑮, the venue of the Expo '86 World's Fair, claims – not without justice – to be the most beautiful of all Canadian cities. It is surrounded by shimmering fjords and snow-covered mountains. The skyline is dominated by skyscrapers that contrast effectively with buildings dating from the beginning of this century, whose copper roofs have grown green with age. The renovated Gastown, bustling Chinatown, elegant Robson Street and the excellent Vancouver Museum are the most interesting attractions.

In Vancouver, nature is always close at hand, for example in the four hundred hectares of Stanley Park situated on a peninsula in front of the inner city. To walk around in Vancouver is to experience nature, be it along walking paths, at picnic sites or when admiring the totem poles, redolent with their history, or – best of all – the superb views. To the north of Vancouver lies the Sunshine Coast: mountain-ringed fjords, where small resorts offer rest and relaxation, rocky coastlines strewn with driftwood, and sunny beaches

Vancouver also has its own Chinatown – one of the city's prime attractions.

all contribute to the beauty of this region. *43*

VANCOUVER ISLAND ⑯, almost five hundred kilometres long and named after the British explorer George Vancouver (1757 – 1798), is the largest island along the west coast. The wild western side of the island has vast forests and frequent rains, while the mild, sunny east coast is ideal for sailing, canoeing and salmon-fishing. Victoria, the capital of British Columbia, lies at the southern tip of the island and delights many visitors with its British colonial atmosphere and – thanks to the warm climate – its luxuriant parks and flower gardens, such as Butchart Gardens.

WINNIPEG ⑰. Founded by fur traders on the Red River in 1738, Winnipeg is a prairie city of around 600,000 residents. Numerous historic buildings have been preserved around Old Market Square in the historic centre of the town. Particularly worth a visit, apart from Winnipeg's excellent museums and galleries, is Lower Fort Garry, thirty kilometres to the north, a Hudson's Bay Company trading fort that has now been restored as a museum village. *31*

MUSEUMS

The best insight into the country's history and culture is provided by its museums, which in Canada numerous and laid out according to the most modern educational concepts. Comprehensive collections are on display in Ottawa's federal museums and in the large museums of each individual capital.

Deserving special mention are the Royal British Columbia Museum in Victoria, the palaeontological Tyrell Museum in Drumheller, Alberta, the Museum of Man and Nature in Winnipeg and the Royal Ontario Museum in Toronto. Virtually every town, no matter how small, has its pioneer museum devoted to interesting episodes from the history of the settlement. Also well worth a visit are the carefully restored fur trading forts, pioneer villages and colonial towns.

LIST OF SOURCES AND ILLUSTRATIONS

Clark Blaise, "A Class of New Canadians," in A NORTH AMERICAN EDUCATION. Toronto: Doubleday and Company, Inc., 1973.

Charles Dickens, AMERICAN NOTES. London: George Routledge and Sons Ltd., 1892.

Wasyl Eleniak, Early Pioneer Memories. From a tape-recording done at the Basilian Monastery, Mundare, Alberta, 1940.

Chief Dan George, "My Very Good Dear Friends," in THE ONLY GOOD INDIAN. (edited by Waubageshig) Don Mills, Ontario: New Press, c. 1970.

Susie Frances Harrison, "Idyl of the Island," in THE OXFORD BOOK OF CANADIAN SHORT STORIES. Toronto: Oxford University Press, 1988.

Harold Harwood, "Fumigating the Map," in THE ATLANTIC ADVOCATE, April 1959.

Beverly Illauq, "Adopting a Culture," in ARCTIC CIRCLE, September 1990.

Margaret Laurence, "The Loons," in A BIRD IN THE HOUSE. Toronto: the Canadian Publishers, McClelland and Stewart Limited, 1970.

Stephen Leacock, "The Marine Excursion of the Knights of Pythias," in SUNSHINE SKETCHES OF A LITTLE TOWN. Toronto: The Canadian Publishers, McClelland and Stewart Limited, 1912.

Edward McCourt, "The Face of Saskatchewan," in SASKATCHEWAN, by Edward McCourt. Toronto: MacMillan Company.

"A Winter Wonderland," in the EDMONTON EXAMINER, 13 January 1991.

We would like to thank all copyright holders and publishers for their kind permission to publish. Despite intensive efforts on our part, in a few cases we were not able to find out who the copyright holders are. Those to whom this applies are asked to contact us.

The map on page 48 was drawn by Fanny Haydee B. Llego.

DESTINATION CANADA
WINDSOR BOOKS INTERNATIONAL, 1992

© 1989 by Verlag C. J. Bucher GmbH Munich and Berlin
Translation: Nicholas H. Lloyd
Editor: Karen Lemiski
Anthology: Carmel Finnan, Karen Lemiski
All rights reserved
Printed and bound in Germany
ISBN 1 874111 00 6